Carol ~
Once in a while,
in an ordinary life,
love gives us a fairytale!
Blessings,
Angela Laura

A RAINBOW IN DECEMBER

– A RAY OF HOPE

By ANGELA ANDREOLI

D1514990

A memoir of a love story
A fairytale

AuthorHouse™
1663 Liberty Drive
Bloomington, IN 47403
www.authorhouse.com
Phone: 1-800-839-8640

© 2010 Angela Andreoli. All rights reserved.

No part of this book may be reproduced, stored in a retrieval system,
or transmitted by any means without the written permission of the author.

First published by AuthorHouse 11/1/2010

ISBN: 978-1-4520-9542-4 (sc)

Library of Congress Control Number: 2010916438

Printed in the United States of America

This book is printed on acid-free paper.

Also by Angela Laura

A Bubble in the Sky
ISBN: 1-4259-1219-2 (sc)

ACKNOWLEDGEMENTS:

PHOTOGRAPHY – *Louise Macca*
                    Frank Andreoli

ANGEL MESSAGES – *Jayne Power*

DEDICATED TO - - -

My Awesome Son - - - FRANK
---who gave me the title of this book …….

My Beloved - - - WALT
---while on earth always encouraged me - - -
---now in spirit, continues to bless me …….

SOME PEOPLE HAVE A GREAT LOVE ONCE IN LIFE – I WAS
FORTUNATE TO HAVE TWO.

Our lives blended in love,
Like the colors of the rainbow

. . . a love story – a fairytale

When someone we love dies, no matter how strong our faith, we are shattered to the core. Many of us start an internal search – asking ourselves and others questions about the after life. Is there REALLY life after we die? Do we, or will we, have interaction with our deceased loved ones? Is life on earth all there is? Is there a heaven? SEARCHING – SEARCHING – SEARCHING for a symbol of hope.

There are many things we can live without, yet, hope is not one of them.

We all need a ray of hope - - - We all need a love story - - -

---and we will meet our loved ones again !!!

On a cold, wintry December morning as we drove on Route 9 going to my dear cousin Joan's funeral we looked up and were blessed by seeing a rainbow right in front of us!!! I have traveled this route for approximately fifty years; this was the first time seeing this sight! Who thinks of rainbows in December in New England? Yet, there it was!

Yes, I believe in signs. Thank You, God, the Source of All Being, for this sign of hope. A statement that for me says life still goes on; it has only changed. Open your eyes to all the signs around you. That is one way we communicate with "the other side." I shared this with the grief-stricken husband and adult children of our cousin Joan.

The rainbow is frequently seen during summer and seldom during winter. To see a rainbow, one has to have rain and sunshine. A rainbow occurs when rain is falling in one portion of the sky and the sun is shining in another. The rainbow has become a metaphor for life! A rainbow is always in front of you while your back is to the sun.

Many people consider rainbows to be an omen of some kind. The legends of many cultures see the rainbow as a kind of bridge between heaven and earth. In Western culture, the rainbow has become a symbol of renewed hope.

The North American Catawba Indians of the Southeast and the Tlingit of the Northwest, whom I met in Alaska, both regard the rainbow as the bridge between the living and the dead. I sometimes cling to this..

We cannot follow the arc of a rainbow down below the horizon. The higher we are above the ground, the more of the rainbow circle we would see. From an airplane in flight, a rainbow will appear as a complete circle with the shadow of the airplane in the center.

Rainbow is also a name given to many organizations. It is also used in the title of many businesses,

After Noah's deluge, the Bible relates that the rainbow gained meaning as the sign of God's promise that life would never again be destroyed by flood. (Genesis 9:13-15) "I have set my bow in the clouds, and it shall be a sign of the covenant between Me and the earth."

The rainbow is one of the beauties of nature.

Historically a rainbow flag was used as a sign of a new era, of hope and of social change. Rainbow flags have been used as a symbol of peace. It is also used to represent friendly businesses or districts.

A rainbow to me is also a symbol of prayer. How often I've said, "Oh God, a rainbow! How beautiful." What is prayer - a communication with God, the expressions of our heart - talking to God about anything, our sorrows, our joys, and listening in silence to God's reply.

When vacationing in the Caribbean we frequently see rainbows. We never fail to get excited; the younger children jumping and dancing around shouting "look, look."

Coming back to Connecticut from the Caribbean, I was looking out of the airplane window; in astonishment, I was seeing the rainbow - a round rainbow!!! In the center of the rainbow was the shadow of the plane!

When we are on land looking up, we only see the horizon and the arc of the rainbow; when we are above it, we look down and see the glorious form of the round rainbow. What an experience!

To witness this part of God's beauty is amazing - something as miraculous.

God's message to me - Life is a circle!!! I am fortunate that I was shown this.

The earth needs rainbows, and so do we

THE FAIRYTALE

I LOVED BEING MARRIED

Being devastated after Sonny's death is an understatement. There doesn't seem to be adequate words to describe how I felt.

I met Sonny when I was thirteen and was married to him for over forty years.

I was told that when it was the right time for another partner to be in my life, I should consult God first.

I was to write down the exact qualities I was seeking in that person - - - AND GIVE THANKS.

God is in charge – my partner is a gift from God

I give God our relationship

My partner is the most valued treasure on the planet

Thank You, God, for manifesting my perfect partner in my life, now.

I want my partner to have/be:
- God consciousness, active truth seeker
- Kind, loving, tender, sincere, loyal
- Generous with self, time and money
- Faithful
- Compatible age
- Refined, intelligent, classy
- Educated
- Unencumbered, working through his stuff
- Similar diet
- Similar interests
- Functional
- Great sense of humor
- Expressive
- Will travel
- Happy and up personality
- Thoughtful
- Gets who I am
- Supportive of me and my work
- Straight communication
- Emotionally available
- Fun loving
- First class taste
- Likes and listens to music
- Open to new ideas
- Cares about people
- Lets his beauty out
- Likes the outdoors
- Likes to read
- Easy to be with
- A holy relationship

At first glance you would never have imagined this was the perfect partner for me for you would have found him sitting on the end seat at the corner of the bar – it was almost his "home away from home." He liked being there because it was the "social club" where friends gathered, brought some samples of home made goods, exchanged recipes, talked about gardening, sports – AND it was the only bar in town with pool tables, two of them! He was on a pool league and wanted to practice. Yea, he also had a Bud bottle sitting in front of him that he nursed, most times very slowly. You might have concluded that he was a drinker.

At one time he owned a Harley. He had tattoos covering his chest, back and arms; he sported a pony-tail and had an ear ring.

He was a classic example of NOT judging a book by its cover.

Let me take off this outer shell and show you the man underneath.

The man I so totally loved!

We met via the computer - - - - - - -

We e-mailed back and forth, "chit-chatting" about little things that grew deeper as we went along. I told him about my late husband, Sonny; how I took care of him the last five years of his life and what we went through starting with colon cancer. I would do it again in a heart beat!

Walt told me that Sonny was in a better place for Walt had suffered a heart attack in which he was clinically dead for six minutes and KNEW there was "something" after the body died. I started to discover Walt's spiritual side. "Walt," I said, "you are WORTHY to get to know." That particular word got to him. We frequently talked about it. He wanted to know how did I come up with and use THAT word. We both believed God gave it to me.

Then one e-mail was different. In it, Walt said he had something to tell me and needed to hear my voice when he said it! He then put down his telephone number on the e-mail and asked me to call him.

What could he possibly say that was of such importance?

Could this be an obstacle before we even get started?

SO.o.o.o I called him. The sound of his voice took my breath away – I loved it! After a few minutes, I asked him, "what's so important?"

"Well," he said, "I have an amputated leg."

"And?" I replied.

He came back with "oh, it turns some people off!"

"OK, well, my Mom had her leg amputated and we still loved her!"

- - - HURDLE ELIMINTED ! - - -

I couldn't get enough of his voice; sometimes we each fell asleep while still being on the phone. When could we meet? He would have to come to me; I had surgery on both feet, got a staph infection from the hospital in both feet, knew real, deep pain, and could not drive.

I waited outside my home for him; I spotted him at the stop sign and my heart did a flip-flop. He told me later, "When I saw you, I thought, oh, God, let that be her!"

He flashed his beautiful smile. Calm down my heart. My world would never be the same.

He came into the house and sat down. We never took our eyes off each other. Within minutes we both knew this time in space was different! We were two wounded souls coming together on a healing journey.

He told me, "talk as much as you want about Sonny, I have room in my heart for his memories."

What a man!!!

He told me a little about his health situation. I said "I don't know if I can do this again – after taking care of Sonny for five years."

"You know," he replied, "the world could blow up tomorrow. Would you consider taking our happiness one day at a time?'

He had me! All we have is one day at a time!

I opened my heart. I learned to receive.

ONE DAY AT A TIME TURNED INTO THREE, INCREDIBLE, BEAUTIFUL, WONDERFUL YEARS!!!!!!!

ADORATION - - -

That first day Walt looked at me with adoration in his eyes. This look just burned itself into my memory. His face just shined with brilliance. For the rest of Walt's life, no matter where we were or what we were doing, he continued to look at me in this adoring way.

- - I CAME FACE TO FACE WITH LOVE - - -

During one of our first talks, Walt asked me, "Is it OK with you to leave the past in the past and make today the first day of our lives and go on from here? Can we start with a clean slate from this day forward? Can we paint this blank canvas?"

"Of course," I said, "works for me!"

- - AND SO ...."WE" BEGAN !!!

We felt clobbered with a vibration that made us feel "Where did that come from?" Truly a case of being bowled over!

YOU ARE WORTHY - - -

Walt was so proud of his two daughters. That very first day he showed me pictures of them. I commented, "Your daughters are stunning!" It was wonderful to find that they are beautiful inside and out.

In a gentle voice Walt said, "they take after their mother."

I felt that this man who spoke so sweetly of his daughters' mother was indeed worthy to get to know. His daughters told me later that Walt discounted his own handsomeness.

Walt also carried a picture of his granddaughter. I loved the expression of love on his face when he looked at it.

INNER VALUE - - -

Over and over Walt told me his Mom and Dad were his heroes. They were the fabric of his life. Walt loved their work ethic and family values. He so thoroughly loved them and was so proud to be their son. Again, he told me over and over that much of what he did and loved to do, was a reflection of what he learned from his parents – cooking, love of gardening, plants and wallpapering from Mom; "Man stuff" especially mechanics, from Dad!!! He beamed with love and pride whenever Mom and Dad were mentioned.

I thank You, God, for these special parents who account for most of the good that was in him; for their examples of warmth, humor and grace. Because of them not only was Walt's life enriched and blessed but so is mine.

HIS BEAUTIFUL SMILE - - -

The first time I went to Walt's home, he was in the midst of an M.S. episode and was using a wheel chair. I was met at the door by Lucy-Belle, Walt's beloved beagle. I saw lit candles and heard soft romantic music – and of course, HIM - - - and his beautiful smile!!!

Little did I know at this first visit that this modular home at the edge of a stone driveway was to become my castle.

The next time I planned to visit Walt, I wanted to surprise him with home cooked meals. I prepared Sheppard's pie, stuffed peppers and a pot of chili. When I arrived at his door, Walt had a shocked look on his face and blurted out, "I thought you couldn't cook!"

I replied, "I said I didn't cook, not that I didn't know how!"

As it turned out, Sheppard's pie was one of Walt's favorite meals.

Another favorite of his was strawberry-rhubarb pie. Fortunately, I was able to do this for him. The best pie I ever made.

He told me that if I had entered this pie in a contest it would take first prize – and he was quite a judge. What appreciation!

When it came time to meet my family, Walt asked if he could meet my son first – privately.

"Of course!"

"Frank, I want you to know that I really love your Mother and she is safe with me. I know I don't need your permission, yet, may I please have your blessing!"

Frank was smiling with joy and proud to be so respected.

WALT WAS AN INCREDIBLY, CLASSY MAN.

Over brunch they bonded. Frank, a professional bass tournament fisherman who got his Captain's license – AND – Walt, an incurable fisherman who made custom fishing rods for people.

From this day forward Walt referred to Frank as Son.

WILL YOU BE MY WIFE FOR THE REST OF MY LIFE - - -

Yes, Yes, Yes, Walt!!!

I like the way you listen
I like the way you respect me
I like your tenderness
I like the way we laugh together
I like your value system
I like that family is important
I like and enjoy your cooking
I feel safe with you
I like your friends
I like that you are open to new ideas
I admire your courage to keep going
I love the way you look when you are with your granddaughter
I like your intelligence
I like the way you look
I like that you are genuine
I like that you do have a deep spiritual side
I like that you show me the real you
I love our connection
I love your magnificence!!!

THANK YOU, GOD, FOR MANIFESTING MY PERFECT PARTNER -

Walt and Angela
invite you
to share in our Joy and celebrate our union,
The Marriage of our Souls.

To love and be loved, is the greatest gift
a heart can ever know.

Yes, we had the gift of age. Our spirits were refined by our unique experiences. We definitely make different decisions at sixty than we did at twenty and forty years of age. We find what is really important and ignore the rest.

We agreed at the beginning of our relationship that if it wasn't oxygen or blood – the rest was trivial.

From the very beginning Walt asked about my interests, pursuits, passions, asking questions about the material being presented. He really listened intently. He got to know me at a very deep level. He loved who I was! He encouraged me to attend lectures and seminars around my field of interests. He read my library of books.

He was open to new ideas. Walt was supportive of all my endeavors. He was thrilled when I found a spiritual group in town that was "just up my alley!" Walt always looked forward to my coming home and sharing what went on. He also attended a few sessions in support of me.

He attended family gatherings and was by my side frequently in all that I did.

Walt couldn't do enough to love me in every way possible.

THE BEST THANKSGIVING EVER !!!

That first thanksgiving was a question – how do we navigate it? We compromised. I went to be with my son and his family. Walt went to be with his parents. We decided that any day we chose would be thanksgiving for us,

So the following Saturday became our feast day!
We went grocery shopping together. Walt insisted that he make all the food preparations and that I be the princess.

He sat me up at a lace-covered table, lit candles and played soft music. I was pampered and made to feel so special.

If anything could possibly be perfect, this was it.

I was giddy with the attention.

He made me feel beautiful.

He left footprints on my heart.

Among his many talents, passions, pursuits and gifts, Walt was a writer – writing articles for magazines. Quite incredible!
I have included a wonderful story he wrote for his granddaughter.

"THE ENCHANTED LAND OF THE PRINCESS NADIA AND THE MOGGS"

By Poppy and Angela

Once upon a time in a far away land, that was surrounded by tall mountains and rushing rivers, there lived a very beautiful young princess Nadia. She lived with her royal parents, the rulers of Moggville, King Serbio and Queen Deilee. They were kind rulers and the princess saw how nice they were to everyone in their kingdom except the evil old MOGGEL. No one was nice to him because he was so mean to all the other people living in the quiet country side. He came out at night when all the people living in Moggville were sleeping and stole all the ferbits and grackles. Everyone was sad because they loved their ferbits and grackles, they were hard to find and even harder to keep if the Moggel found out about them.

Some people thought he could smell them and that was how he knew where they were and other people were sure if he could hear them when they purred like a kitten, but it really didn't matter how he knew, he just knew how to find them and when he found one he just snatched it up and carried it back to his cave on the darkest side of the highest mountain in Moggville. No one really knew where his cave was and everyone was afraid to look for it. This bothered Princess Nadia, or "Noddy" as her grandfather and Angela liked to call her, because Noddy liked watching the ferbits and grackles playing together and tumbling about, in the tall grasses surrounding their castle playing hide and seek. So one warm summer day Noddy asked her mom, the Queen, if she, Noddy, could play outside in the sun. "Sure Noddy," the

Queen replied, "but stay close to the castle. We just heard of another ferbit missing." Instantly a frown came across her face, which was very unusual, for Noddy was known far and wide as always having the brightest smile in all of Moggville. Everyone knew Noddy had a magical gift with her smile, making everyone who saw it happy and nice to each other.

So Noddy grabbed her backpack, filled with her favorite toys and headed outside, through the heavy doors and across the bridge over the little stream that ran past the castle, bubbling through the rocks as it trickled by. This was one of Noddy's favorite places to play. She liked to float leaves downstream and dream of where they would land. This was also where she liked to throw little pieces of bread to the fish that lived in the stream, laughing every time one would come up to slurp it in. "Hi Fishy," she would shout every time one would rise to eat the bread, thinking she could hear them saying "thank you, Noddy." This was a wonderful place to play. There were salamanders who changed colors and pollywogs swimming about, growing their legs like their older brothers and sisters, the bright green frogs, who peeked out of the water at her, just floating on the surface and watching her play. Now, the night before it had rained, hard, so the quiet little stream was running higher and louder than usual, making it hard to hear all the usual stream noises. Noddy was surprised when she heard a soft squeaking sound coming from under the bridge. Because Noddy played there so much she was familiar with all the sounds of the stream so she was surprised to hear the soft squeaking coming from under the bridge. WHAT is that she wondered as she walked carefully towards the bridge, watching where she put her feet on the still wet stones and slippery mossy spots.

Arriving at the bridge she noticed it was dark beneath it, so very dark she couldn't see, but the squeaking continued, getting a little louder as she got closer. Remembering her mother telling her about the missing ferbit she wondered if that was what she hearing. But Noddy had heard ferbits and greckles noises all of her life. They were common and were always making their own noises and sure didn't sound like this sound. Kneeling down on a patch of soft moss Noddy noticed a small ball of fur, holding on to one of the large rocks under the bridge, but it was still too dark to see what it was and it was just a little too far for her to reach. How can I help it she first wondered, and then looking around she noticed a long branch next to the path she was on. Maybe, if I slide the branch to it whatever it is will grab it and I can pull it out of the water, she thought. AND SURE ENOUGH, it did. Whatever it was held onto that branch tightly as Noddy began to pull it out from under the dark wet bridge. When she finally got it out of the darkness and into the sunlight Noddy was so surprised to see a very wet shivering brown and white ball of muddy fur with a black stripe of fur around its' big brown eyes and just as soon as it neared the shore – POP, right into Noddy's arms it jumped. At first she was scared when it did that but she just kept holding the wet little fur ball until it stopped shaking and squeaking while she began to look closely at it. The more she looked at it the more the little animal relaxed and Noddy began to smile her magical smile, telling her new little friend "it's okay now, you are safe with me."

"What are you and why are you under the bridge?" she asked as she tried to lay it in the warm sun. But the little ball of fur was shivering so much it just held on to her arm. Noddy had so many questions to ask her new friend, " do you live here in Moggville? Why were you under the bridge? What's your name?" But no answers came out of its' now smiling mouth. I KNOW, Noddy said to herself, I will ask Mommy what it is and can I keep it? Picking up her backpack, she carried a muddy wet whatever in through the castle doors shouting, "MOMMY, MOMMY COME HERE QUICK AND SEE WHAT I FOUND!!!" Hearing her daughter yelling, the Queen quickly rushed to Noddy. "What is it Noddy, what are you so excited about?" And then she saw what Noddy was holding. "OH MY GOODNESS, NODDY," was all she could say.. Then she saw how wet and muddy Noddy was and told her "wash up and change your clothes and then I will tell you what you have there." Noddy rushed upstairs and washed and changed her clothes faster than ever before because she was so curious about what she had rescued and just as quickly rushed back to her mother. The Queen was sitting with and listening to all the different noises her little friend was making.

"Mommy, what is it? Can I keep it? I found it under the bridge." Taking a deep breath, the Queen said, "Noddy, what you found is a VERY RARE, VERY SPECIAL animal called a ROLLO-JOLLEE, and I have only seen one once before when I was with your Auntie Bee. They are suppose to have magic powers and bring good luck and happiness to anyone who finds one; and yes, you may keep it. BUT since you found it you will have to take care of it." "YAHOO!" yelled Noddy, "I will call him RJ."

Noddy will learn all about RJ and his special skills as they have lots of adventures together.......

The amazing aspects of this man just kept coming. He believed bees are very important to mankind. At one point in his life, Walt was a beekeeper. We went out to get a bee cylinder (like a small hive) to put near the garden. The bees came and made it their home.

Walt also put out bird feeders so I could watch the many species that came to our yard; woodpeckers, cardinals, blue jays, hummingbirds, etc; a kaleidoscope of color. I was thrilled!

HE ALWAYS DID HIS BEST TO MAKE ME HAPPY.

On a Caribbean vacation our group was huddling under "our" hut. I was lying down on the chaise lounge with Walt sitting next to me on a chair. He reached over to get some lotion and told me to put my feet on his lap. Was this a dream? He gave me the absolutely best foot massage I have ever had! Every woman there was jealous.

MY SHOW-OFF!!!

One of our vacation stops was the island of St. Thomas. While there we took a side trip to the island of St. John's.

When we got on the boat to start our adventure the sky was very interesting. As the vessel pulled away from the dock the sky was dark, ominous and it started to rain – ONLY ON ONE SIDE! On the other side of this small craft the sun was shining!

WHAT A METAPHOR FOR LIFE!!!

We are on this life journey and we have a choice; we can chose to look at either side and make that our experience. We will still get to the end no matter what choice we make; only we decide which way we want the experience to be.

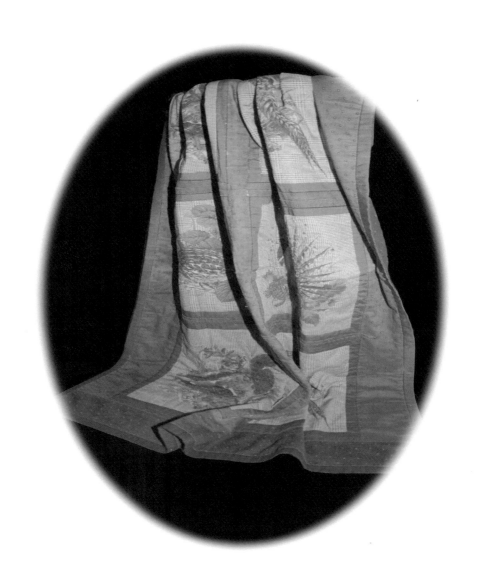

Getting home from anywhere and spotting me in the doorway, produced this incredible smile from Walt. The smile would just melt me.

Watching him belly laugh was a gift. I would just look at him and say, "you are so handsome!"

Sometimes I would sit on the sofa watching him do "whatever" and my heart would just soar!

In my world, he was perfect in my eyes and in my heart!!!

I had a small medical procedure – minor surgery. On arriving home, Walt had me lie down and lovingly covered me with a blanket his Mom had made. To him it symbolized covering me with his love and the love of his mother!
In my turn, when Walt fell asleep in the recliner, I would put his Mom's blanket in the dryer, then cover him with the warmth! He loved and appreciated this. It was my pleasure to spoil him in anyway that I could.

WORDS JUST DON'T CAPTURE THE SACRED LOVE WE SHARED.

We were best friends. We loved to be with each other. We laughed and laughed especially at ourselves. We are pretty funny characters if we really look at ourselves.

We took such delight in each other's presence. I loved being with him – to doctors' appointments, the hardware store, oil changes for the truck, home supply stores, buying him sneakers, even to go to the dump was exciting. I was with HIM. I never tired of it.

Walt was fun in an easy, soft way. He laughed so easily.

Walt never needed to be told to do anything. If the rubbish needed to be taken out, he NOTICED and just did it. When the kitchen floor needed waxing, he would beat me to it (unless I did it while he was sleeping.)

Walt loved to cook stir-fry. We went grocery shopping together; and we went to many different places besides the local grocer – each time and place was a great adventure; cooking stores for gadgets, getting a pot rack for near the stove, specialty items stores, little "out of the way" places for spices (oh, how he loved spices). The state of Connecticut became our food playground. He even engaged a few men to shop for him to bring back certain foods.

If I went grocery shopping by myself, I had to promise Walt I would leave the grocery bags in the car for him to bring in (except the refrigerated items.) I especially had to leave the heavier items.
There was an ease and elegance in our love – it was a journey home. It was passion!

Passion for a new life awakening.

A DREAM!

He would come into the house from the garden. He loved his garden and took great pride in it.

After doing his best to shake the dirt off his shoes, there was still some clinging to them. I would not ask him to remove the shoes – he needed the support to stand and walk. He would apologize. I said, "that's what they make vacuum cleaners for!" He would take the vacuum away from me, glad to do that chore. In the scheme of things this was not important; honoring each other in the relationship took precedence.

In order to make the home property nicer for me, he dragged small boulders from around the yard to make a border. He had ingenuity at how he accomplished this. He got one of his large plastic bins, made a hole near the top to put a rope through for a handle, put the bin on its side, rolled a bolder into it and dragged it where it was needed.

There wasn't enough he could do to make me proud to be where I was living. He then put in flowers and plants to border the walkway, driveway and front of the house.

Walt made me window boxes for parsley and basil with its' fragrance greeting us at the front door.
On the small, front deck he built especially for me as a wedding gift, we would share a cup of tea or coffee together with the sun shining on us. On the front of the deck he put up a sign he engraved, "PRIVATE – RESERVATIONS ONLY" – Our very own special place.

I got a sliver one day from the wood railing – that just wouldn't do! He made sure that would not happen again. He devised a metal railing from something he had in the yard – a testament of his love to me!!!

Yes, our love and time together was intense; somewhere, underneath, I now know we were trying to beat the clock – doing our best to get it all in.

When I would get a haircut, my hair done for an occasion or a manicure, Walt made sure, as soon as he saw me, to acknowledge what was done. "Come here, Sweetheart, and let me see!"

Books were Walt's friends; he liked most authors, old and new; his interests wide and varied, no subject off limits. He was brilliant and humble. Walt liked classical music; we would listen to his favorite while he cooked, so proud to let me into his world.

Walt introduced me to Bluegrass music!!! I loved it! I had preconceived notions about this "kind" of stuff – not nice either. We took the RV to one festival for four days. Another time found us sitting in the pouring rain in ponchos with umbrellas over us. What die-hards we were. I was bursting with excitement. WOW – thank you, Sweetheart, for new adventures.

I was never a "groupie" – now in my older years, here I was! We followed a band that played Irish music. (The Corby's) Every time we were with them, they played "Whiskey in the Jar" and dedicated it to Walt. We did our best to be where ever they were – UP – HAPPY – ALIVE !!!

Where have I been all of my life?

WALT KEPT OPENING NEW WORLDS FOR ME SHOWING ME NEW HORIZONS

There was a reverence between us. We honored each other and said frequently "you are a blessing to me!" We knew we had a holy relationship and acknowledged it. We came together as part of God's family. Most days began with us participating in the TV Mass. The spiritual side of our being became deeper and deeper.

Walt had a Bible on the table in front of the sofa. It was respected; nothing could go on top of it. It was "consulted" frequently.

Walt received a Bible when he was nineteen years old. Even at this age the gospels of St. Matthew was his favorite. I feel he is talking to me now by what he underlined; what was most important to him. Walt was an altar boy until he was seventeen years old. Most people did not know this side of him – a deep, strong and gentle love of God.

We had two favorite times of day - - -

1.) In the late afternoon – talking as we shared a cup of tea . ...
2.) As we got ready for sleep – talking, sharing and praying.......

We had a little ritual with each other; I would say "thank You, God, for this man!"

He would say "thank You, God, for this woman and thank you, Sonny."

When he first said "thank you Sonny," I asked Walt why he did that. He replied, "your being with Sonny helped make you who you are, so I have to say thank you to him."

We were like two kids out to play – gourmet jelly beans (and they had to be "Jelly Belly's) became part of our night-time ritual. I would close my eyes as he reached into the jar for two of them, one he put in my mouth and I had to guess the flavor – he had the other one! (Buttered popcorn flavor became my favorite)

We operated on the level of love.

I LOVED HOW HE LOVED ME.

"I LOVE THIS WOMAN"
Walt never stopped telling me and the world that he loved me. As we crossed Main Street in town, he would stop and shout, "I love this woman!" If Walt were at the local bar (the one we called the social club), or if we were in a restaurant, he would get up and announce "I want everyone here to know that I love this woman!"

One day as we stood face to face, him holding me gently, Walt told me one disappointment, regret he had was that he couldn't have children with me; he would have loved that! I felt and saw the love pouring from his heart and his eyes.

Looking into his eyes let me know without a doubt that he loved me - - -
UNCONDITIONALLY!!!

HIS LOVE GAVE LIFE MEANING.

WALT, IN SO MANY WAYS, YOU WERE OUR GIFT FROM HEAVEN!!!

ALWAYS A SWEETHEART

He was definitely not an ordinary man!!!

Walt had integrity and compassion; he had the gift of listening intently. He was the champion of the "underdog." He knew how to keep a secret. If anything was told to him in confidence, that's where it stayed.

Walt was self-giving. His gifts to others were given quietly; when he saw a need, he did his best to fill it. He asked for no acknowledgment nor recognition.

He was romantic, warm, loving, fun – cared about other people, loyal, could be counted on, kept his word, intuitively keen, a true person in every way, liked to laugh and laughed easily, loved new ideas, not afraid to take chances.

Even though there were two TV sets in the house, we were respectful of each other about the TV programs we watched as we wanted to stay together in the same room.

Walt believed pampering was good for the total person – body, mind and soul! An exciting gift he gave me and his daughter (he felt bonding was important, too!) was a day at a spa! How glorious our world was.

THE R V

Up until now, when I went on vacation, I used a key or card to get into the room and our accommodations were all set.

Welcome to the world of camping and the RV. In my wildest imagination I couldn't conceive of the work and knowledge it takes to have and run an RV! I was literally in awe of Walt. Only those who have been there can understand the scope of what needs to be done and the knowledge to do it!

Yes, a book can be written just of this experience alone; and movies have been made!

We bought an older model. His working on the RV felt like Christmas time to me – the tree and home being decorated, and the final picture being presented to "OOH and AHH" over!

The fixing up of the vehicle was an offer from the depths of Walt's being. He brought it to me – giving me a gift – watching me with a gleam in his eye for my expressions! He was so happy to be doing this for us.

I was deeply concerned for him to be doing ALL this work. I honestly thought it was too much an undertaking for Walt. Yet, there he was in all his glory doing it!

ALL IN THE NAME OF LOVE. THE DEPTH OF HIS BEING KNEW NO BOUNDS!

ONLY GOD KNOWS THE EFFORT HE EXPANDED - - -

One night Walt's granddaughter came to visit and wanted to be in the house on wheels! Her request was for the lights to be off; in the dark with flashlights nearby, lying on her chosen cot, she wanted to hear scary stories. Oh, what a night! It was worth having the camper if only to have this one experience!

Lucy Belle was Walt's beloved beagle. He said to me, "this is her house, she just allows us to live in it!"

Her strong presence illuminated the home.
They were definitely meant for each other; it was the reason before I entered their world, that Walt went home.

I had never had a pet, so again, a new experience! Walt and Lucy Belle so generously shared their love of each other with me, encircling me into their tight-knit world.

Lucy's place at night was on the bed with Walt; she also "owned" this space. Then I came along.

Lucy would get up on the foot locker (the bed was high) and put her paws on the bed, looking up at us with her soulful eyes. Walt would turn to me and say, "is it OK for our daughter to come on up?"

"Sure, bring her on!"

Only those who experienced it know how a pet could quickly become like "your child."

LUCY BELLE BROUGHT LIFE TO THIS LITTLE CORNER OF THE WORLD - - -

Excruciating pain from the amputated leg ripped through Walt's body 24/7. Boy, how he disliked his false leg. He was in constant phantom pain yet he needed the prosthetic to keep his balance – that and the beautiful cane he and God created.

The main part of the cane came from a spiraling grapevine; he cut it to the size he needed then went to a home supply store for the bronze ball he attached on the top; it was constantly noticed and comments were made on how unusual and great it looked.

Many times people offered to buy it!

Walt also suffered from MS. He had difficulty walking especially on uneven surfaces.
He never used any of this as an excuse to not do his best at all times.

He didn't TRY his best, he DID his best!

There is a difference!!!

A LESSER MAN WOULD HAVE GIVEN UP LONG AGO.

Walt was always a gentleman. He insisted on opening the car door for me, or any door, no matter what!

I knew his taking extra steps sometime were extremely painful – yet, he ALWAYS went above and beyond all expectations.

HIS PRECIOUSNESS - - -
   HE HAD A BEAUTIFUL LIGHT!!!

Walt was a man who refused to quit – when other men would have.
The image of this man has to be admired.

I SALUTE YOU, WALT!

ALL THAT TRULY MATTERS IN THE END IS THAT YOU LOVED!

I am standing upon the seashore, a ship at my side, spreads her white sails to the morning breeze and starts for the blue ocean. She is an object of beauty and strength. I stand and watch her until at length she hangs like a speck of white cloud just where the sea and sky come to mingle with each other. Then someone at my side says "There she is gone." Gone where? Gone from my sight. That is all. She is just as large in mass and hull and spar as she was when she left my side and she is just as able to bear her load of living freight to her destined port. Her diminished size is in me, not in her and just at the moment when someone at my side says "There she is gone" there are other eyes watching her coming, and other voices ready to take up the glad shout "Here she comes."
And that is dying.

   ---Henry Van Dyke

Every now and then, God puts an angel in front of us in/on our path.

Walt had a massive heart attack on September 5th, on Saturday of Labor Day weekend.

During the time he was in the hospital and hospice suspended between heaven and earth I received several messages from him as spoken through my friend, Jayne Power.

He crossed over on October 17, 2009.

WALT IS AT HOME WITH GOD!!!

September 10, 2009

A message from the Angels as spoken through Jayne Power.

We want you to know that Walt wants to speak. He is traveling all over. He is enjoying the freedom of being without his body for a while. He has been traveling every chance he gets. When he has company (in the hospital) he is in his body and he hears everything that is going on around him. He feels the love and he knows that he is not ready to cross over yet. He still has work to do on the physical plane yet he wants you to know that he is really enjoying being pain free and able to walk or fly without that "darn leg" (prosthetic). He wants you to know Angela "I love you and the joy you have brought to my life. I want to continue to bring that same joy to your life."

"Angela, I have seen the light this time!!! And, Jayne, you should see all the angels, they are everywhere- thousands of them!!! Angela, I am well taken care of. I am so happy to be having this chance to visit the other side by seeing clearly now. Stay strong, My Love, and be patient. I am with you in your heart and you are in my heart. Your love is what heals me. Thank you for loving me. I am a better man because of you. I will be next to you in spirit for a while. Take care of yourself. I love you."

September 21, 2009

A message from the Angels as spoken through Jayne Power.

Walt is talking. "Angela, I am here. I want you to know that I am so proud of the way you are handling this situation that I have put you in. I am sorry. I love you so much and I was so proud to have you by my side. You have made the last few years of my life, the best years of my life. I was not a perfect man yet I felt perfect in your eyes. You never judged me like the others. You loved me for who I am and I thank you for that. I was able to find peace where I thought there was none. You are truly my angel and I shall always love you. I want you to know that now that I have been able to experience life on the other side, I know now why you had great faith. It is amazing being free of that old body. I can go anywhere and experience everything I want with just a thought. I wish I had been able to do that with the camper and I'm sure you do too!!! Yes, it was aggravating but it brought me joy to do it for us. Angela, don't be mad at the camper (and I truly was!). I am glad we were able to experience the Cape together in that way. It was worth it for me."

"I want you to be brave tomorrow and know that you are giving me my wish." (taking him off the ventilator) "I have already acclimated myself to the other side so there will be no problem with my transition. It will be easy – easier than getting that camper up the hill! Ha! Ha!!!"

"One thing you must always remember, my love for you was and is real! I have never loved another like I love you. Please, please don't allow anything or anyone to diminish the love I have for you. It is real. We will see each other again, you can be assured of that. All that you have spoken to me about and tried to get into my thick skull is real. Angela, there is no death. I am with God, angels and loved ones, like you said. I was never judged or condemned – only loved.."

"It is a beautiful place. You see the big picture and boy is it big! I can't even convey to you all that I have experienced; it is all good. Love me and remember the WE that we were."

"I am free of pain and pills and bad memories. Now I only choose to take with me the love. Nothing more matters now, Angela."

"Angela, just take the love and hold it in your heart. I will always be there."

October 13, 2009

A message from the Angels as spoken by Jayne Power.

Walt is speaking. "Hi Hon, I am so much more in love with you now than you could ever imagine. I know you think that I don't know who you are when you are with me but I want you to know that the tired old soul that you have been feeding and crying over is the shell of who I was. I am whole now, Angela. I have been spending the majority of my time on the other side. Angela, I AM HOME! I want you to know that I still love you more than I have ever loved another – I will carry that love with me for eternity. We were together before and we will be together again in a different way. I want you to know that all you need to live is love. Your love made my life worth living. Thank you, My Love."

"I need you to explain all this to the girls, Angela, and tell them I am so proud of the women they have become. I know I was not the best Dad because I was always very wrapped up in my problems but I did the best I could under the circumstances. Please tell them I love them and that I will always watch over them. I hope they choose to remember the man that I was these last three years because of you."

"Angela, please tell Mom and Dad I will be waiting for them when it is time to cross."

"I wanted to hang on a little longer so you could get used to the idea of me crossing. I wanted to give those I love a chance to say goodbye in their own private way. I have been truly blessed, Angela, to have such wonderful people in my life. I see it all so clearly now; that is another reason why I chose to stay around; I needed to see for myself. I know now that my life was full of meaning and everything I went through happened for the reason of soul development. Do you know that the more difficult a life, the more the soul evolves!!! I am happy to see this life come to an end."

"Angela, you still have many to bestow your blessings to – you have plenty of love left to give. I will always be in your heart. I will not make you go through this much longer. Thank you for your patience and love. I will be here to talk when you need me. I love you."

WALT LEFT EARTH FOUR DAYS LATER

November 9, 2009

A message from the Angels as spoken through Jayne Power.

God wants you to know, Angela, that your pain is felt over the loss of Walt and many others in your life. You are also to know that you still have much to do in this lifetime. You have spent a lifetime learning, now it is time to teach to others what you have learned. Once your life is in order again, teach, Angela! You can help many the way you did help Walt and Sonny. Help those who want to learn; they are your best students – they are very receptive. Angela, it is your calling. You are needed to help spread God's word. You are the gift that Walt has bestowed on those who you have come to call your friends.

Walt wants to speak. "Angela, I love you more now than ever! Thank you for all that you are doing and have done, all in the name of love for me! I know now that we were brought together as part of God's Divine plan. Everything that happens in life happens for a reason and to teach. There are no accidents – you know that already!"

"I am sorry that I left you such a mess to clean up. Angela, I know you feel so alone and overwhelmed. Learn from this process you are going through now. Try and look at it as a gift."

"I watch Mom and Dad – they seem to be doing OK. Everyone seems to be moving along – and you, My Darling, must also – doing what you know. Angela, you must live what you know."

"We will see each other again – I can assure you of that."

"It is so simple here – no bills, no pills, no doctors!!! Only Love. Live life simply – love all – even the ones that so thoroughly upset you. I am telling you this – we are all made out of the same God energy, even them! You can love their soul, you don't have to love who they are in this incarnation. They are in your life as a learning opportunity. Let them go with love."

"I am so happy here, Angela. Please don't think of me as a poor soul who lived a tormented life; remember, Angela, I chose that life. Remember the hardest lives are rich in food for the soul. I was never hungry!!! Ha, Ha!!!"

"Angela, I see all. I know you are hurting. Please, Angela, remember our love – it never dies. Angela, keep loving all of us over here; we can feel it. I have so many who love me here also. It turns out that Sonny and I have been together in many lifetimes. Angela, just do what you do best! Love, Love, Love – and teach what you know – it is your gift to humanity – it is your gift to yourself!"

"I will be by your side anytime you need me. Try and feel my energy; it will get stronger with time. I can hear you also. Talk to me, Angela. Spend your time living the human experience.

You will be in spirit again. Physical life is a gift from God, don't waste it."

"I love you, Angela. Thank you for teaching me how to love unconditionally. I will always be in your heart. Talk to me again any time you are feeling lonely. I will help you like you helped me."

I BELIEVE WE DO COME INTO CONTACT WITH THE OTHER SIDE AND THIS IS ONE OF THE WAYS IT HAPPENS FOR ME.

Are they just co-incidences? I don't believe so; I feel co-incidence is an occasion where God wishes to remain anonymous.

I was driving out of the hospital garage a few days before Walt was transferred to hospice. I said out loud, "Sonny, we need help – from your vantage point in heaven; would you please send it to us." Just then a small pick-up truck pulled out in front of me with the license plate "422" – Sonny's birthday!!!

I know he heard and answered me.

I had the Catholic TV channel on and a cartoon came on. This was Christmas Eve day morning. A character came on and announced, "Hi, my name is Walter, and some people call me Wally!"
Walt was called Wally in his younger years; Wally was also the pen name under which he wrote.

It was 10:30 p.m. I was guided to turn on the TV and on a certain channel; the program was "House." The female patient in the program said, "the man's name is Walter." Dr. House said, "oh, my grandfather Walt!"

Walt died on October 17th – on what would have been Sonny and my wedding anniversary. The three of us are forever connected.

I choose to believe that Walt knew in his subconscious that his health was going downhill fast and wanted to spare me; he did not want me to take care of him. So as a last act of love – left earth!.

Now, I ask Walt to let me know of his presence by me finding heart shaped stones/rocks. I've already amassed a basket full!!!

The moment that you died,
My heart split in two,
One side filled with memories
The other died with you.
I often lay awake at night
When the world is fast asleep
I wander through the memories
With tears upon my cheeks
Remembering you is easy
I do it everyday
Yet missing you is a heartache
That never goes away
I hold you tightly within my heart
And there you will remain
Life has gone on without you
Yet it will never be the same.

     ---anonymous

My good-bye letter to Walt - - -

My Dearest Walt – My Beloved, My Sweetheart, My Lover - - -

Right now I am in the most inconsolable moments of my life. I can only see life through my tears, I am not angry with you, just with life that this has to happen. I feel cheated! I feel as if a huge part of me has died. My heart feels raw. I am happy for you that you are out of pain and in that wonderful place with God. I am lonely without you. I am lost without my faithful friend.

You know I can take care of myself yet it is not the same. I pray that God, very soon, will enable me to fully accept His will for my life including this loss.

I miss your magnificent person so much. The night you collapsed, my world went with you. How do I get the picture out of my mind of that fateful night.

I didn't have enough time with you. I am grateful that I did have you and your love.

You gave me a fairytale.

I love and admire you so much; the more I learn of you, the more I love and admire you. Thank you for loving me.

You made me feel so special and beautiful. I loved being in your presence. Our time together was intense. I now realize that we had to get a lifetime in only three short years.

I know we both felt it was divinely inspired.
I am having such difficulty letting go.

There were so many things I still wanted to do with you – state parks, beaches, a cruise, museums, books to share – the list goes on and on.

I want that last kiss, that last hug, that last "I love you." I want! I want! I want! Please help me to say good-bye for now. I know I'll "see" you on the other side.

The ache in my heart is crushing, unending. I did not know how hard it would be to say good-bye. I want to lash out! I want to just stamp my feet and yell "NO, NO, NO!!!"

I regret my future won't have you physically in it. How can I just pour out what is in my heart. I know that I didn't really lose you, yet I did in physical form.

I know it is selfish of me to want you so much. I don't want to say good-bye yet I know I have to!

In saying good-bye please promise me I will still feel your energy. Please let me feel you holding my hand. Please promise me you will help me write "our" book.

I'll do what I need to do, yet I look forward to the time we're together again. Your light, Walt, was and is beautiful. It still shines in my heart! We opened such an array of new horizons for each other.

Good-bye for now, my Sweetheart. I love you. Your love for me knew no limits!!!

CROSSING THE BAR - - -
Sunset and evening star,
And one clear call for me!
And may there be no moaning of the bar,
When I put out to sea
But such a tide as moving seems asleep,
Too full for sound or foam,
When that which drew from out the boundless deep
Turns again home.
Twilight and evening bell,
And after that the dark!
And may there be no sadness of farewell,
When I embark;
For tho' from out our bourne of Time and Place
The flood may bear me far,
I hope to see my Pilot face to face
When I have crossed the bar.
------- Alfred Lord Tennyson

Lovingly recited (from memory) by Walt's 90 year old Dad at the cemetery, on the day of burial

NOTES TO EACH OTHER –

Angela - --
I know when the woman I love arrives home smiling as always and is always happy to see me. The house feels as if it takes a deep breath and flushes all the day's tension away – while we share our cup of tea together as we were always meant to be.

Walt - - -
I know I've found a soul-mate, a twin flame, a true partner! I have found that person who loves me, who makes me happy, who fills me with a deep sense of belonging, one who makes me feel completed. I am at home in you.

Walt - - -
You are like a diamond-my diamond! The facets unlimited. Our time together helps me to know more of you – a precious gem - as one facet at a time is revealed. All these facets make the diamond sparkle!!!

Angela - - -
I want to tell you Happy Valentine's Day (and Happy Every Day) and how much I truly love you. You are my world.

Hi Sweetie - - -
It's just me. I just wanted to make sure that I told you that I love you.
I'm here waiting for you.
You have me.
I love you, Sweetheart!

a message from Walt when I went out – left on my cell phone

I still have it today!

Do you wonder sometime as you're walking through time,
What life is all about
Do you sing in the rain when you're hurting with pain
And really want to shout!
Yet life is a gift – take one day at a time
To do with as you please
Pray and give thanks for all that you have
That comes blowing on you like the breeze!
- - composed by Ann DiBacco

THERE IS NO RIGHT OR WRONG WAY TO DO GRIEF

FEEL THE HURT – YOUR PAIN IS REAL

DON'T CRY BECAUSE IT'S OVER - - -
SMILE BECAUSE IT HAPPENED.
------- Mother Theresa

May the sun always shine on your window pane
May a rainbow be certain to follow each rain

and until we meet again,
May God hold you in the hollow of His hand.......
-------Irish Blessing

ABOUT THE AUTHOR

As far back as she can remember, Angela has felt a spiritual field around herself: it is still evident in her life today.

Angela is a graduate of the Silva Method of Mind Development. She has a CT license for Therapeutic Massage Therapy. She is a Reiki Master/Teacher of the Usui lineage. She is an Ordained Minister.

Angela lives in CT near her son. She is surrounded by a very large family and many friends.

LaVergne, TN USA
10 November 2010
204227LV00001B